GAME OF SKILLS

From Curiosity to Mastery

DUSHYANT BHATT

For more Information
Game-of-Skills.com

INDIA · SINGAPORE · MALAYSIA

ISBN 979-8-89610-301-1

*To curious minds and lifelong learners – may this book
guide you on your journey to mastering the skills
that will shape your future.*

*And finally, to every individual who dares to
step outside their comfort zone and take accountability
for their own growth: this book is for you.
Keep pushing boundaries, stay curious, and never stop evolving.*

Contents

Acknowledgments

Writing this book has been an incredible journey, and it would not have been possible without the support, guidance, and encouragement of many people.

First and foremost, I want to thank my wife and daughter for their endless support and patience. Your belief in me has been my driving force, and I am grateful for your constant love and encouragement.

A heartfelt thanks to my parents, my mentors, colleagues, and friends who have shared their wisdom, insights, and experiences with me over the years. Your guidance has been instrumental in shaping the ideas in this book, and I am deeply appreciative of your generosity.

I would also like to acknowledge the leaders and thinkers whose work has inspired me. The concepts explored by experts in personal development, leadership, and skills mastery have been a foundation for this book, and I am grateful for the knowledge they have shared with the world.

To my readers, thank you for embarking on this journey with me. It is my hope that this book will empower you to take ownership of your growth and inspire you to pursue mastery in every aspect of your life.

Lastly, a special thank you to everyone who believed in this project and helped bring it to life. Your support has been invaluable, and I am honored to have had you by my side during this process.

Thank you all.

Introduction

The Shift to Practical Skills in Today's World

In today's rapidly evolving world, success is no longer measured by the number of degrees or certifications hanging on your wall. While formal education lays the foundation, it is your ability to apply knowledge through practical skills that truly sets you apart. We're living in an age where the rules of the game have changed, and those who understand the importance of adaptability, hands-on learning, and continuous improvement are the ones thriving.

The purpose of this book, *Game of Skills*, is to shed light on the critical role that practical skills play in achieving growth, success, and sustainability in both personal and professional lives. Whether you are a fresh graduate, a mid-career professional, or even a seasoned expert, the message remains the same – your ability to acquire, develop, and master real-world skills will define your journey.

Why Practical Skills Matter More Than Ever

In the past, having a degree from a reputed institution was often seen as the ticket to a successful career. However, as industries continue to be disrupted by technological advancements, automation, and global competition, the gap between what is taught in classrooms and the actual demands of the workforce has widened. Theories and textbook knowledge, while important, are no longer enough to guarantee success.

The digital revolution has fundamentally shifted the landscape. Jobs that didn't exist a decade ago—such as data scientists, UX designers, and AI specialists—are now critical to the functioning of companies across the world. What ties these roles together? It's not just knowledge; it's the practical ability to solve problems, create, adapt, and think critically in an ever-changing environment.

Today's economy rewards those who can translate theory into action, people who are problem-solvers, creators, and doers. As industries evolve at lightning speed, possessing the right skills can mean the difference between staying ahead of the curve and being left behind.

The Disconnect Between Education and Real-World Skills

Many education systems, especially traditional ones, focus heavily on rote learning and theoretical understanding. This creates a significant disconnect between what students learn and the skills they need to excel in the real-world. Colleges may teach you how to analyze a business case, but they don't often teach you how to lead a project team through a challenging situation or how to communicate effectively with different stakeholders.

The ability to work in dynamic environments, solve complex problems, manage time efficiently, or lead a team–these are the practical skills that come from real-world experience, not just from sitting in a lecture hall. These skills are what employers are actively searching for, and they are often the key to unlocking career advancement, entrepreneurship, and innovation.

A World That Rewards Doers

The workforce of the future belongs to those who are willing to learn by doing. Practical skills not only make you more employable but also open the door to opportunities that others may miss. The ability to adapt and continuously learn is the single most powerful asset you can develop.

In this book, you will discover how you can identify the skills that matter most, acquire them, and leverage them for success. Whether you're learning to code, mastering communication, or honing your leadership abilities, the practical application of these skills will drive your growth.

The world doesn't just need people with knowledge – it needs people who can execute. This book will guide you through the process of becoming a "doer" – someone who isn't just armed with information but knows how to use it to make things happen.

Why I Wrote This Book

My own career journey has taught me that practical skills are the foundation of success. I've seen firsthand how real-world experience can accelerate growth and open doors that may seem out of reach. Through my work across various industries—from technology to leadership—I have always prioritized learning by doing. I've built teams, scaled products, and navigated challenges by relying on hands-on experience, not just theoretical knowledge.

As I began mentoring professionals and students, I realized there's a growing need to focus on this concept: practical skills are the ultimate game-changer. This book is my attempt to share the insights I've gathered, the lessons I've learned, and the strategies that can help you succeed in this "Game of Skills."

What You'll Learn in *Game of Skills*

In this book, you will explore a comprehensive framework for identifying, developing, and applying practical skills. Here's what you can expect:

1. **Understand the Importance of Skills**: We will start by understanding why practical skills are more relevant now than ever before, particularly in the face of rapid technological changes and shifting job markets.

2. **How to Build the Right Skills**: You'll learn how to assess which skills are most valuable for your industry, how to acquire them effectively, and strategies for continuously improving and updating your skills.

3. **Develop a Growth Mindset**: To succeed in today's world, you need to foster a mindset that embraces learning, challenges, and even failure. I'll share insights into how to cultivate this mindset to fuel your personal and professional growth.

4. **Apply Skills for Maximum Impact**: Learning skills is only half the battle–you must know how to apply them to get results. You'll discover ways to translate your knowledge into action, create measurable success, and turn challenges into opportunities.

5. **Prepare for the Future**: Finally, we'll explore the skills that will be most in-demand in the future and how you can future-proof your career by staying adaptable and proactive in your learning journey.

The Game Has Changed–Are You Ready to Play?

Game of Skills is not just a guidebook; it's a call to action. Whether you're just starting your career or looking to pivot in a new direction, the practical skills you develop will define your success. The world is moving faster than ever, and the ability to adapt, learn, and grow through hands-on experience is essential.

So, are you ready to play the game? If so, this book will show you how to equip yourself with the tools and skills needed to win.

1

The Rise of Practical Skills

In an era where the landscape of industries is constantly evolving, one thing remains clear: practical skills are no longer optional–they are essential. The world of work has undergone dramatic shifts in recent years, driven by rapid technological advancements, globalization, and changing workforce demands. The old paradigm, where a degree was considered the ultimate achievement for career success, is being disrupted. Today, possessing real-world, practical skills is what sets successful individuals apart.

This chapter will explore the historical context of this shift, the reasons behind the growing importance of practical skills, and how individuals and organizations are adapting to this change.

The Historical Shift: From Theoretical to Practical

For decades, a formal education and a degree were considered the keys to a successful career. Universities and colleges were seen as the gatekeepers of knowledge, and companies would primarily recruit based on academic credentials. But as industries have evolved, especially with the rise of technology and digital transformation, the workplace has demanded more than just theoretical knowledge. Employers need individuals who can apply that knowledge in real-world scenarios, solve problems, and adapt to rapidly changing conditions.

Historically, industries were less reliant on fast-paced technological changes. Many jobs had a clear and defined path, and the skills needed could be taught once and remain relevant for decades. For example, a mechanical engineer or accountant could rely on the same set of principles throughout their careers, with minimal updates. However, the arrival of the digital age disrupted this stability.

The 21st century brought about unprecedented changes. Today, job roles are constantly evolving, and skills that were considered niche just a few years ago, like coding, data analysis, and digital marketing, are now mainstream. The half-life of skills—how long a skill remains relevant—has shortened dramatically. As technology continues to advance, industries like artificial intelligence, blockchain, and automation are not just emerging—they're becoming essential.

The Growing Importance of Practical Skills

In today's world, success is increasingly tied to your ability to execute and perform in real-world situations. This shift has placed practical skills—hands-on abilities that can be directly applied to solve problems and create value—at the forefront.

1. **The Digital Revolution and Automation**

   The ongoing digital revolution has accelerated the need for practical skills across every industry. Automation, AI, and machine learning are replacing many routine tasks, especially those that require repetitive knowledge work. In this environment, practical skills such as creativity, problem-solving, emotional intelligence, and adaptability have become indispensable.

   For instance, companies today are looking for individuals who not only understand concepts like machine learning but can also implement algorithms, analyze large datasets, and make actionable recommendations based on that data. Theoretical knowledge is simply not enough anymore–what truly matters is the ability to execute.

2. **Startups and the Entrepreneurial Boom**

   The rise of startups and entrepreneurial ventures has also placed a spotlight on practical skills. Entrepreneurs, by necessity, need to be skilled in multiple areas–marketing, finance, product development, and team management. In such fast-paced environments, individuals must not only understand the theory behind business but also wear multiple hats and execute strategies quickly and effectively.

   Many successful entrepreneurs and startup founders did not come from traditional business backgrounds. What they did have, however, was a strong set of practical skills honed through experience. They knew how to pivot, how to test ideas rapidly, and how to build something from the ground up. These are skills that can't be taught solely in classrooms – they are learned in the field, through trial and error.

3. The Gig Economy and Freelance Culture

The gig economy and freelance culture have further cemented the value of practical skills. In the freelance world, clients hire based on your ability to deliver results, not based on where you went to school. The ability to show a portfolio of work, demonstrate specific competencies, and adapt to different projects is what drives success in this space.

Today, freelancers and gig workers are thriving in industries like graphic design, content creation, software development, and consulting because they offer specific, tangible skills that businesses need immediately. Their value lies in what they can do, not just in what they know.

The Limitations of Traditional Education

Traditional education systems often fail to equip students with the real-world skills they need to thrive in a modern workforce. Many universities continue to emphasize theoretical learning, memorization, and standardized testing, focusing on knowledge acquisition rather than the ability to apply that knowledge in practical ways.

While degrees and certifications can demonstrate a baseline understanding of a subject, they don't necessarily show that a person has the practical skills needed to succeed in a job. This disconnect has become increasingly apparent to both employers and job seekers. According to recent surveys, a large percentage of employers believe that graduates are not fully prepared for the workforce, citing a lack of critical thinking, problem-solving, and communication skills.

Moreover, the world of work is evolving much faster than educational institutions can keep up with. By the time a student graduates, much of what they have learned may already be outdated. The rapid development of new tools, platforms, and technologies means that staying relevant requires continuous learning and adaptation–something traditional education does not always encourage.

The Role of Lifelong Learning

In response to this gap, there has been a growing emphasis on lifelong learning and continuous skill development. People are realizing that to remain competitive, they need to constantly acquire and hone new skills. This is where practical skills come into play.

Lifelong learning isn't just about taking courses or attending workshops. It's about applying what you learn, experimenting, and iterating. It's about learning by doing. Whether you are learning a new programming language, improving your leadership abilities, or mastering the art of negotiation, the ability to apply those skills in real-world settings is what will make you stand out.

In addition, the rise of online platforms like Coursera, LinkedIn Learning, Udemy and others has democratized access to practical skill-building. These platforms offer a range of courses that are often taught by industry professionals who bring real-world experience into the learning environment. As a result, learners can acquire highly relevant skills at their own pace and apply them immediately.

How Companies Are Adapting

Organizations are also recognizing the importance of practical skills and adapting their recruitment and development strategies accordingly. Many companies have shifted their hiring practices to focus less on formal education and more on demonstrable skills. This is especially true in the technology sector, where practical skills can be more valuable than traditional qualifications.

For example, many companies have moved away from requiring a college degree for certain roles, instead focusing on candidates' abilities to solve problems, think critically, and innovate. Additionally, many organizations are offering internal training programs and mentorship opportunities designed to help employees develop practical skills on the job.

Businesses that prioritize practical skill development not only have a more capable workforce, but they are also better positioned to navigate challenges and capitalize on new opportunities.

Conclusion: The New Economy of Skills

As we move deeper into the 21st century, the value of practical skills will continue to grow. Whether you're an aspiring entrepreneur, a professional looking to advance your career, or a student entering the workforce for the first time, your ability to execute, adapt, and innovate will be your most important asset.

This chapter has explored the rise of practical skills and the forces driving this shift. The remainder of this book will dive deeper into how you can identify, acquire, and apply the practical skills that will help you succeed in the "Game of Skills." It's time to embrace the power of doing–because in this new economy, actions truly speak louder than words.

2

Why Degrees aren't Enough

For generations, earning a degree was seen as the golden ticket to success. Society conditioned us to believe that a university education guaranteed a stable, well-paying job and a clear path to career growth. However, as industries rapidly evolve and new technologies emerge, the job market is showing us a different reality. Degrees, while still valuable, are no longer the sole determinant of career success. In this chapter, we will explore why degrees alone aren't enough in today's world and how practical skills are now the key to unlocking growth and opportunity.

The Degree Dilemma

Traditionally, a university degree symbolized a well-rounded education and a deep understanding of a particular subject. It was the benchmark for employers to assess a candidate's potential. Yet, despite the prestige associated with degrees, many graduates today find themselves struggling to translate their academic knowledge into real-world applications.

A growing body of research reveals that many graduates feel unprepared for the workforce, citing a gap between what they learned in classrooms and the skills required in their chosen careers. Employers echo this sentiment, with many expressing frustration over hiring candidates with impressive academic backgrounds but lacking the practical skills needed to perform on the job.

The challenge is that the world is changing faster than traditional education systems can adapt. By the time students graduate, much of what they learned may already be outdated, particularly in fields driven by technology, where innovation happens at breakneck speed.

Why a Degree Is No Longer the End Goal

1. The Rapid Evolution of Technology

Technology is advancing at an unprecedented rate, and industries across the board are being transformed. New tools, platforms, and frameworks are constantly emerging, rendering older methods and techniques obsolete. A degree that focused on technologies from even 5 years ago may not be relevant today. Practical skills, on the other hand, evolve with real-world applications and are constantly updated through experience and hands-on learning.

2. The Skills Gap

There is an increasing gap between what educational institutions teach and what the market demands. While degrees provide foundational knowledge, they often fall short in areas like critical thinking, communication, leadership, and problem-solving skills that are essential for navigating the complexities of modern workplaces.

3. Shift Toward Outcome-Based Hiring

Companies are becoming less concerned with academic credentials and more focused on what a candidate can actually deliver. Outcome-based hiring is on the rise, where employers prioritize the ability to solve problems, demonstrate competency, and achieve results. Many industries, particularly tech, now value practical skills and experience far more than a formal education. Coding boot camps, for example, are becoming increasingly popular because they focus on outcomes–teaching students the skills they need to build products and solve problems right away.

Degrees and the Knowledge Illusion

One of the biggest misconceptions perpetuated by traditional education systems is the "knowledge illusion"–the belief that having academic knowledge is sufficient to succeed in a career. While degrees offer valuable theoretical frameworks and help students build a foundation, they often do not teach the critical skills needed for applying that knowledge in practical, real-world settings.

For instance, a graduate in computer science may understand the theory behind algorithms but may not have experience writing efficient code under pressure, collaborating with a team, or dealing with real-world bugs and software crashes. Similarly, a business administration major may know the principles of management but may not know how to lead a diverse team through conflict or implement a strategy in a fast-paced startup environment.

Academic environments often focus on passing exams, writing papers, and adhering to a rigid curriculum. However, in the real-world, success requires adaptability, collaboration, creative problem-solving, and the ability to handle ambiguity. These are the skills that degrees alone cannot provide.

The Rise of Skills-Based Learning

In response to the limitations of traditional education, there has been a shift toward skills-based learning. Skills-based learning emphasizes the development of practical, job-ready skills through real-world experience and hands-on practice. This approach is gaining traction because it addresses the immediate needs of both individuals and employers.

1. **Microlearning and Boot Camps**

   Skills-based programs, such as coding bootcamps, design sprints, and microlearning platforms, have become popular because they focus on teaching practical skills in a condensed timeframe. These programs are designed to equip learners with the specific abilities they need to enter the workforce quickly and make an impact.

   For example, a coding bootcamp might teach digital marketing, design, programming, data structures, and full-stack development in just a few months, providing students with practical, usable skills that can immediately be applied to real-world projects. Similarly, microlearning platforms break down complex topics into bite-sized lessons, allowing learners to build skills progressively and on demand.

2. Mentorship and Apprenticeships

Apprenticeships and mentorships are also experiencing a resurgence in popularity. These programs pair learners with experienced professionals who provide hands-on training, real-world insights, and the opportunity to learn by doing. This form of learning is invaluable because it allows individuals to gain practical experience while being guided by experts who have already navigated the challenges they will face.

Mentorship programs, in particular, are a powerful way for professionals to develop the nuanced, soft skills that are often hard to teach in a classroom. A mentor can guide you through complex decision-making processes, teach you how to communicate effectively in the workplace, and help you build the confidence to tackle bigger challenges.

Practical Skills: The Key to Employability

Employers today are less interested in where you went to school and more concerned with what you can actually do. In a competitive job market, the ability to demonstrate practical skills is often the deciding factor between landing a job and being passed over for someone more capable.

1. Skills Outweigh Degrees in Hiring Decisions

In a survey conducted by LinkedIn, 89% of hiring managers stated that they prioritize practical skills over degrees when making hiring decisions. The rise of portfolios, coding challenges, skill assessments, and practical interviews reflects this shift.

2. Portfolios and Proof of Work

In many industries, especially in creative and technical fields, having a strong portfolio of work is more important than any degree. Portfolios allow candidates to showcase their skills and accomplishments through tangible proof, whether it's a coding project, a design portfolio, or case studies demonstrating problem-solving abilities.

A candidate with a well-documented portfolio demonstrating their ability to execute real-world projects will stand out far more than someone with a degree but no practical experience. It's this ability to "**show, not tell**" that employers value most today.

Degrees vs. Skills: Bridging the Gap

It's important to note that degrees and practical skills don't have to be mutually exclusive. A degree still holds value in providing foundational knowledge, developing discipline, and signaling a commitment to education. However, the key to success is combining a degree with real-world skills. Those who can bridge the gap between academic knowledge and practical application are the ones who will thrive in today's job market.

For those currently pursuing a degree or considering one, the goal should be to augment formal education with as much hands-on experience as possible. Internships, freelance work, side projects, and online courses are all ways to gain the practical skills that complement theoretical learning.

1. **Internships and Side Projects**

    Internships are one of the best ways to gain practical experience while still in school. They allow you to apply what you've learned in a real-world environment, work alongside professionals, and build the skills employers are looking for. Side projects—whether it's building a website, creating an app, or starting a blog—are also excellent ways to demonstrate initiative and practical skill development.

2. **Online Learning and Certifications**

    In addition to internships, online learning platforms provide access to a wide variety of courses that focus on practical skills. Many platforms offer certifications in everything from programming languages to digital marketing and project management. These courses are often taught by industry experts and allow learners to build job-ready skills at their own pace.

Conclusion: The Balance of Knowledge and Skills

As the workforce continues to evolve, the value of practical skills will only increase. While degrees provide a solid foundation, they are no longer sufficient on their own. In today's world, the most successful individuals are those who continually build and refine their practical skills through experience, hands-on learning, and a willingness to adapt.

This chapter highlights the growing gap between formal education and the skills needed in the workforce. In the next chapter, we'll dive into the anatomy of practical skills – what they are, why they matter, and how to start building them to stay competitive in the modern economy.

3

Mastering the Skill Mindset

In a world where practical skills are the cornerstone of success, having the right mindset is equally essential. The "**Skill Mindset**" isn't just about learning specific abilities; it's about cultivating a mental framework that encourages continuous growth, adaptability, and resilience. This chapter will dive into what it means to develop a Skill Mindset, why it is critical to long-term success, and how you can cultivate this mindset to master new skills and navigate an ever-changing world.

The Concept of the Skill Mindset

The Skill Mindset is the mental framework that prioritizes learning through doing, embracing challenges, and seeing failure as a stepping stone rather than a setback. It is a combination of a growth mindset—where you believe that your abilities can be developed through dedication and hard work—and a commitment to lifelong learning.

Having a Skill Mindset means understanding that expertise is not static but constantly evolving. No matter where you are in your career or life journey, there is always room to grow, improve, and develop new abilities. This mindset is what enables people to thrive in rapidly changing environments and make the most of their practical skills.

Why the Skill Mindset Matters in Today's World

We are living in an era of constant change. Whether it's technological advancements, evolving industries, or shifting economic landscapes, the ability to adapt is more critical than ever before. The Skill Mindset equips individuals with the mental agility to navigate these changes and capitalize on new opportunities. Here's why it matters:

1. **Continuous Learning is Key to Staying Relevant**

   Skills that are in demand today may become obsolete tomorrow. For example, technological developments in automation, artificial intelligence, and digital platforms have revolutionized industries in ways no one could have predicted even a decade ago. The Skill Mindset encourages individuals to keep learning, upskilling, and reskilling throughout their lives, making them more resilient to changes in the job market.

2. **Challenges Are Opportunities for Growth**

   People with a Skill Mindset see challenges not as threats, but as opportunities to learn and grow. They understand that the path to mastering any skill is filled with obstacles, and instead of avoiding these hurdles, they tackle them head-on. This mindset fosters resilience and persistence, 2 essential traits in mastering any skill.

3. **Adaptability is the New Superpower**

   Adaptability has become one of the most sought-after traits in today's job market. Being adaptable means you can apply your skills to new situations, learn from feedback, and adjust your approach when things don't go as planned. A Skill Mindset ensures that you're not only open to change but thrive on it.

Growth Mindset vs. Fixed Mindset

The foundation of the Skill Mindset is rooted in the concept of the Growth Mindset, a theory popularized by psychologist Carol Dweck. According to Dweck, individuals typically operate from one of 2 mindsets: the Growth Mindset or the Fixed Mindset.

1. **The Fixed Mindset**

   In a Fixed Mindset, people believe that their abilities, intelligence, and talents are set in stone. They tend to avoid challenges because they are afraid of failure, viewing it as a sign of incompetence. People with a Fixed Mindset are more likely to stick to what they already know, resisting change and growth.

2. **The growth mindset**

   In contrast, the growth mindset is the belief that skills and intelligence can be developed over time through hard work, learning, and perseverance. People with this mindset embrace challenges, learn from mistakes, and see effort as a pathway to mastery. The Growth Mindset is foundational to the Skill Mindset because it encourages individuals to continuously learn and improve, regardless of where they start.

Building the Skill Mindset: Practical Strategies

Developing a Skill Mindset requires conscious effort and a commitment to change. The good news is that anyone can cultivate this mindset with the right strategies. Here's how you can build and nurture a Skill Mindset:

1. **Embrace Lifelong Learning**

   Lifelong learning is the cornerstone of the Skill Mindset. It means making a habit of learning new things, whether through formal education, online courses, mentorship, or hands-on experience. Successful individuals view learning as an ongoing process, not something that ends when they leave school or reach a certain career milestone.

   Actionable Tips:

   - **Read Every Day**: Whether it's books, articles, or blogs, reading helps you absorb new information and perspectives.

   - **Enroll in Courses**: Take advantage of online learning platforms to pick up new skills.

   - **Stay Curious**: Approach every situation with curiosity. Ask questions, seek out new knowledge, and challenge your assumptions.

2. **Adopt a Beginner's Mindset**

   One of the most significant barriers to growth is the belief that you already know everything. The Skill Mindset requires humility and the willingness to approach situations as a beginner. This mindset keeps you open to new ideas and methods, even if you're already experienced in your field.

Actionable Tips:

- **Be Open to Feedback**: Seek out constructive criticism from peers, mentors, and colleagues. Don't view feedback as a judgment of your abilities but as a tool for improvement.

- **Try New Things**: Take on projects or challenges that push you outside your comfort zone. Being a beginner again helps you develop resilience and adaptability.

3. **Learn from Failure**

Failure is an inevitable part of learning any new skill, yet many people fear it because they see it as a reflection of their worth. People with a Skill Mindset understand that failure is not a roadblock but a learning opportunity. Every setback provides valuable insights into how to improve and do better next time.

Actionable Tips:

- **Reframe Failure:** Don't see failure as the end of the road. Instead, ask yourself, "What can I learn from this?" Reflect on the experience, identify areas for growth, and use the lessons learned to try again.

- **Take Calculated Risks:** Push yourself to take risks that will help you grow. Even if you fail, you'll gain experience that will make you more skilled in the future.

4. **Set SMART Goals**

To cultivate a Skill Mindset, it's important to set clear, measurable, and achievable goals for your skill development. Without goals, it's easy to lose focus and become complacent. Setting SMART goals— Specific, Measurable, Achievable, Relevant, and Time-bound— provides structure to your learning process and helps you stay motivated.

Actionable Tips:

- **Be Specific:** Instead of setting vague goals like "I want to learn coding," be specific: "I want to learn JavaScript and complete 5 coding projects in the next 3 months."

- **Break It Down:** Break larger goals into smaller, actionable steps that you can work on daily or weekly.

- **Track Your Progress:** Regularly check in with yourself to see how far you've come. Adjust your goals as needed to keep yourself on track.

5. **Surround Yourself with Like-Minded People**

Your environment plays a significant role in shaping your mindset. Surrounding yourself with people who are also focused on growth and learning can help keep you motivated and inspired. Whether it's a mentor, a peer group, or an online community, being around others with a Skill Mindset reinforces your commitment to continuous learning.

Actionable Tips:

- **Join Communities:** Find online or offline groups where you can engage with others who share your passion for learning and growth.

- **Network with Growth-Oriented Individuals:** Seek out mentors or peers who have a Skill Mindset and can provide support, encouragement, and accountability.

The Role of Resilience in the Skill Mindset

Resilience is the ability to bounce back from setbacks, adapt to change, and keep going despite challenges. It's a critical component of the Skill Mindset because the journey to mastering a skill is rarely smooth. There will be failures, frustrations, and moments of doubt. What sets successful individuals apart is their ability to persevere in the face of adversity.

1. **Developing Mental Toughness**

   Mental toughness is the resilience to keep working on a skill even when progress is slow or results aren't immediately apparent. It's the ability to push through discomfort, uncertainty, and doubt.

   Actionable Tips:

   - **Practice Delayed Gratification**: Understand that mastering a skill takes time and effort. Resist the urge for immediate results and focus on long-term gains.

   - **Celebrate Small Wins**: Acknowledge and celebrate the progress you make along the way. Every small step brings you closer to mastery.

2. **Managing Stress and Avoiding Burnout**

   While it's important to stay committed to your skill development, it's equally important to manage stress and avoid burnout. A Skill Mindset includes knowing when to step back, recharge, and approach challenges with renewed energy.

   Actionable Tips:

   - **Take Breaks**: Don't overwork yourself in pursuit of mastering a skill. Take regular breaks to rest and rejuvenate your mind.

   - **Prioritize Self-Care**: Exercise, meditate, and engage in activities that help you relax and reset.

Conclusion: Mastering the Skill Mindset for Long-Term Success

Mastering the Skill Mindset is not a one-time effort; it's a lifelong journey. It's about cultivating a mentality that embraces growth, resilience, and continuous learning. In a world where the only constant is change, the ability to learn and adapt quickly is the most valuable skill of all.

The Skill Mindset will empower you to not only develop practical skills but also to navigate challenges, stay relevant in a rapidly evolving world, and achieve long-term success.

4

Building Personal Skills Toolkit

In today's fast-paced and dynamic world, having a well-rounded personal skills toolkit is essential for both personal and professional success. Your toolkit is a collection of the skills you develop over time, customized to meet the demands of your career, industry, and life goals. The process of building this toolkit isn't just about acquiring random abilities –it's about intentionally identifying, developing, and refining skills that align with your aspirations and market needs.

In this chapter, we will explore how to identify the most valuable skills for your toolkit, practical ways to acquire these skills, and strategies for honing them to mastery. By the end of this chapter, you'll have a roadmap for building a strong personal skills toolkit that you can leverage for growth, career advancement, and long-term success.

What Is a Personal Skills Toolkit?

A personal skills toolkit is essentially a collection of hard and soft skills that you've developed, which enable you to perform effectively in your chosen field. Unlike static knowledge, your skills toolkit is dynamic and evolves over time as you encounter new challenges, opportunities, and industries.

1. **Hard Skills vs Soft Skills**

   Your toolkit will typically be composed of 2 types of skills: hard skills and soft skills. Hard skills are specific, technical abilities that are often measurable. Examples include coding, data analysis, or financial modeling. These are typically acquired through formal education, training, or hands-on experience. Soft skills, on the other hand, are interpersonal and cognitive abilities that enable you to navigate social and professional environments effectively. Examples include communication, leadership, critical thinking, and adaptability.

The most effective toolkits combine both types of skills, as they work in tandem. For example, being an excellent software developer (hard skill) won't be as impactful if you can't communicate your ideas clearly to your team (soft skill).

2. **The Importance of Transferable Skills**

Transferable skills are those that can be applied across multiple roles, industries, and situations. These are especially valuable because they give you the flexibility to adapt to new roles or career changes. Examples of transferable skills include problem-solving, project management, and teamwork.

As you build your skills toolkit, focusing on transferable skills will give you an edge in a competitive job market, allowing you to pivot and thrive in various industries or roles.

Identifying the Most Valuable Skills for Your Toolkit

The first step in building your personal skills toolkit is identifying which skills are the most valuable for your career and goals. This requires a thoughtful analysis of your current position, where you want to go, and the demands of your industry.

1. **Conduct a Skills Audit**

A skills audit is a self-assessment process where you evaluate your current abilities and compare them to the skills needed to achieve your goals. By doing this, you can identify gaps in your skills and focus on areas that need development.

Actionable Tips:

- **List Your Current Skills**: Write down the skills you already possess. Include both hard and soft skills, as well as any certifications or qualifications you've earned.

- **Identify Gaps**: Compare your skillset to the demands of your industry or your career goals. What are the key skills that you need but don't yet have? This will give you a roadmap for what to focus on.

- **Ask for Feedback**: Seek feedback from peers, mentors, or supervisors about your strengths and areas for improvement. External perspectives can provide valuable insights into skill gaps you may not have noticed.

2. **Research Industry Trends**

Industries are constantly evolving, and the skills that are in high demand today might not be as relevant tomorrow. Research the current and future trends in your industry to understand which skills will be most valuable in the long run.

Actionable Tips:

- **Follow Industry Publications and Blogs:** Subscribe to industry news sources, blogs, and thought leaders to stay informed about changes in your field.

- **Attend Webinars and Conferences:** These events often highlight emerging trends and technologies, giving you insights into what skills are becoming essential.

- **Network with Industry Professionals:** Talk to people in your industry about the skills they are prioritizing and how they are staying competitive.

3. **Align Skills with Your Career Goals**

Once you have a clear understanding of industry trends and your own skill gaps, it's time to align the skills you want to develop with your long-term career goals. Think about where you want to be in the next few years. What roles, responsibilities, and achievements do you envision for yourself? Then, identify the skills that will get you there.

Actionable Tips:

- **Set Specific Career Goals**: Clearly define what success looks like for you in the future. Are you aiming for a leadership role, entrepreneurial success, or a career change?

- **Map Skills to Goals**: Determine which skills are essential for achieving those goals. For example, if you want to become a project manager, skills like communication, time management, and leadership should be high priorities.

Acquiring New Skills: Practical Strategies

Now that you've identified the most valuable skills for your toolkit, the next step is to acquire them. There are many ways to build skills, ranging from formal education to on-the-job experience.

1. **Learn by Doing**

   One of the most effective ways to develop practical skills is through hands-on experience. Whether you're learning a technical skill like coding or a soft skill like public speaking, real-world practice is essential for mastery.

   Actionable Tips:

   - **Take on Projects**: Seek out opportunities at work or in your personal life to apply new skills. If you're learning graphic design, for example, offer to design flyers for a local nonprofit or create marketing materials for a friend's business.

   - **Start Side Projects**: Side projects give you a safe space to experiment and learn. Whether it's building a personal website, launching a podcast, or developing an app, these projects will help you put theory into practice.

   - **Freelance**: Freelancing is an excellent way to gain experience in a new skill while also earning money. Platforms allow you to take on short-term gigs that align with your skill development goals.

2. **Leverage Online Learning Platforms**

   Online learning has revolutionized how we acquire skills. Online platforms offer thousands of courses on a wide variety of topics, from coding, communications, and data science to leadership.

   Actionable Tips:

   - **Set Learning Goals**: Before starting a course, define your learning objectives. What specific skill do you want to acquire, and how will you apply it?

- **Choose Industry-Recognized Certifications**: Many online courses offer certifications that can add credibility to your skills. Focus on certifications that are recognized and valued in your industry.

- **Practice Consistently**: Learning a skill online is just the first step; make sure to practice what you've learned regularly to retain the information and build proficiency.

3. **Seek Mentorship**

   Mentorship can be one of the most powerful ways to build skills. A mentor can offer guidance, share their own experiences, and help you avoid common mistakes in your learning journey.

   Actionable Tips:

   - **Identify Your Learning Gaps**: Be clear about what skills you want to develop before seeking a mentor. This will help you find someone who aligns with your learning needs.

   - **Reach Out to Industry Experts**: Don't hesitate to ask for mentorship from professionals you admire. Whether it's through LinkedIn or networking events, many successful individuals are willing to share their knowledge.

   - **Join a Mentorship Program**: Some organizations offer formal mentorship programs where you can be matched with a mentor based on your goals and needs.

4. **Formal Courses or Certifications**

   For certain industries or technical skills, formal education and certifications are necessary. **Actionable Tips:**

   - **Research Industry-Recognized Certifications**: Before investing time and money into a course, ensure that it's recognized and respected in your field.

   - **Balance Theory with Practice**: While formal education is valuable, it's important to also apply what you're learning in practical situations to truly internalize the skills.

Mastering Skills: Strategies for Refinement

Acquiring a skill is only the first step. To truly master it, you need to continually refine, practice, and push yourself to new levels of proficiency.

1. **Practice Deliberately**

   Deliberate practice is focused, purposeful, and aimed at improving specific aspects of a skill. It's more than just repetition – it involves setting specific goals, seeking feedback, and constantly pushing yourself to improve.

   Actionable Tips:

   - **Break Skills into Components**: Identify the individual elements of a skill that you want to improve. For example, if you're learning public speaking, focus on one aspect at a time such as tone, pacing, or body language.

   - **Seek Feedback**: Don't be afraid to ask for constructive criticism from others. External feedback can highlight areas you might not notice on your own.

   - **Set Specific Improvement Goals**: Each time you practice, set a goal for what you want to improve, whether it's increasing your speed, improving accuracy, or gaining confidence.

2. **Embrace Lifelong Learning**

   Mastery of any skill requires a commitment to continuous learning. Even if you become proficient in a skill, there's always more to learn as new trends and techniques emerge.

   Actionable Tips:

   - **Stay Updated on Industry Trends**: Subscribe to industry journals, blogs, and attend conferences to stay informed about the latest developments in your field.

   - **Challenge Yourself Regularly**: Once you've become comfortable with a skill, push yourself to take on more challenging projects or roles that require you to apply the skill at a higher level.

Conclusion: The Power of a Well-Rounded Skills Toolkit

Building your personal skills toolkit is an ongoing journey that requires intentionality, persistence, and adaptability. By identifying the most valuable skills for your goals, acquiring them through practical learning, and refining them to mastery, you create a toolkit that empowers you to succeed in any environment.

As you continue to develop your skills toolkit, remember that it's not just about collecting as many skills as possible – it's about selecting the right skills that align with your long-term vision and goals. In the next chapter, we'll explore how to apply these skills in practical, real-world scenarios to drive growth and success in your career.

5

Applying Skills for Growth

Acquiring practical skills is only half the battle. The real power of a skill comes from your ability to apply it effectively in real-world scenarios. Whether you are aiming for career advancement, starting a business, or simply improving yourself, applying your skills strategically is the key to driving personal and professional growth.

In this chapter, we'll explore how to leverage your skills to achieve tangible results, unlock new opportunities, and fuel continuous development. You'll learn how to align your skills with your goals, measure the impact of your skillset, and adapt your approach as you grow. By the end of this chapter, you'll have a clear understanding of how to use your skills as tools for success in any area of life.

Why Applying Skills is Crucial for Growth

Many people spend time acquiring skills but fail to apply them in ways that yield significant results. In the fast-moving landscape of modern industries, possessing skills without applying them effectively is like owning tools but never using them. Mastery lies in practice, and growth comes from strategically implementing what you know in real-world situations.

1. **Turning Knowledge into Action**

   Knowledge alone isn't enough to drive change or success – it's the application of that knowledge that makes an impact. For instance, knowing how to code doesn't have much value unless you can use that knowledge to develop functional software, solve real-world problems, or contribute to a larger project.

   Skills give you the ability to execute ideas, complete tasks, and create value. Growth occurs when you regularly apply your skills in meaningful contexts, such as improving workflows, solving complex problems, or driving innovation in your organization.

25

2. **Gaining Confidence and Competence**

   Applying your skills consistently helps build both confidence and competence. The more you apply what you know, the more proficient you become and the more comfortable you'll feel tackling bigger challenges. This is especially important in industries that demand rapid adaptation and hands-on experience.

   Applying skills also helps solidify your learning. You move from theoretical understanding to practical knowledge, where the skill becomes second nature.

3. **Creating Measurable Results**

   Employers, clients, and collaborators value results. The ability to apply your skills effectively enables you to deliver measurable outcomes, whether it's increasing sales, improving efficiency, launching a product, or solving a critical issue. Results speak louder than qualifications, and demonstrating real-world impact will set you apart in any field.

Aligning Skills with Personal and Professional Goals

To apply your skills for growth, you first need to align them with your personal and professional goals. This requires a clear understanding of what you want to achieve and how your skills can be utilized to make progress toward those objectives.

1. **Define Your Growth Goals**

   Before you can apply your skills strategically, you need to clearly define what growth looks like for you. Are you seeking career advancement? Do you want to start a business? Or are you focused on personal development, such as improving communication or leadership abilities?

   Actionable Tips:

   - **Set Clear, Specific Goals**: Whether your goal is to get promoted, build a business, or lead a new initiative at work, be specific.

- **Break Down Your Goals**: Break your goals into smaller, actionable steps. If your goal is to grow in your career, identify the skills that are most relevant to achieving that, such as project management, negotiation, or team leadership.

2. **Identify Skills That Drive Your Goals**

Once your goals are clear, the next step is identifying the specific skills you need to develop or apply to achieve those goals. If your goal is career advancement, focus on the skills most valued in your industry or within your organization. If your goal is personal growth, focus on the skills that will help you overcome personal challenges or improve your abilities in specific areas.

Actionable Tips:

- **Prioritize High-Impact Skills**: Not all skills will have the same level of impact on your goals. Prioritize skills that will yield the most significant results.

- **Match Skills with Opportunities**: Align your skills with upcoming projects, tasks, or roles that can help you advance.

Applying Skills in Real-World Contexts

Applying skills effectively means using them in ways that solve problems, create value, and achieve goals. Here are practical strategies to ensure that your skills translate into real-world success.

1. **Solving Problems with Your Skills**

One of the most valuable ways to apply your skills is to solve problems, whether it's in your personal life, workplace, or business. Problem-solving demonstrates your ability to think critically, use creativity, and deliver results that matter.

Actionable Tips:

- **Identify Problems You Can Solve**: Look for challenges in your environment - whether it's an inefficiency at work, a client's unmet needs, or a personal hurdle - and apply your skills to solve them.

- **Create Solutions, Not Just Ideas**: Problem-solving requires action. Move beyond identifying issues and take steps to develop and implement solutions.

- **Measure Your Impact**: Once you've applied your skills to solve a problem, evaluate the outcome. Did your solution save time, reduce costs, or increase performance? Quantifying your impact will help you measure your growth and show others the value of your skills.

2. **Leveraging Your Skills to Add Value**

Applying your skills effectively means leveraging them to create value for others, whether it's your employer, your clients, or your community. Value can take many forms, including improved processes, innovative solutions, or increased revenue.

Actionable Tips:

- **Offer Your Expertise**: Don't wait for people to come to you with opportunities. Be proactive in offering your skills where they are needed. If you're an expert in digital marketing, offer to revamp your company's social media strategy, even if it's not part of your official job description.

- **Look for Gaps and Fill Them**: Identify gaps in your team or organization where your skills can make a difference. For instance, if you notice that your company's customer service could be improved, take the initiative to implement a new system or process.

- **Deliver Results Consistently**: Consistency is key when applying your skills. Delivering value repeatedly helps build trust and solidifies your reputation as someone who can get the job done. Whether it's completing projects on time or driving measurable improvements, make sure your work speaks for itself.

Measuring the Impact of Your Skills

To grow, you need to assess the effectiveness of your skills in real-world applications. By measuring the impact of your skills, you can refine your approach, double down on what works, and continuously improve.

1. **Use Key Performance Indicators (KPIs)**

KPIs are metrics used to measure your performance and the outcomes of applying your skills. They help you track progress and identify areas where you can improve. For example, if you're applying leadership skills, KPIs might include team performance, project completion rates, or employee satisfaction.

Actionable Tips:

- **Set Measurable Outcomes**: For every skill you apply, define specific outcomes you want to achieve.

- **Track Progress Regularly**: Keep an ongoing record of how your skills are contributing to results. This might be through weekly or monthly reports, personal reflections, or tracking specific metrics such as revenue, customer satisfaction, or project completion rates.

2. **Seek Feedback and Reflection**

Sometimes the impact of your skills isn't immediately visible, which is why seeking feedback from others is crucial. Feedback from colleagues, clients, or mentors can provide valuable insights into how effectively you're applying your skills and where you can improve.

Actionable Tips:

- **Ask for Constructive Criticism**: Don't shy away from asking for honest feedback. Whether you're leading a project or learning a new technical skill, ask for specific feedback on how you can improve.

- **Reflect on Your Own Performance**: In addition to external feedback, reflect on how well you believe you're applying your skills. Ask yourself questions like, "What worked well? What didn't? How can I apply this skill better in the future?"

Adapting Your Skills for Continuous Growth

As you apply your skills, you'll encounter new challenges, feedback, and evolving industry trends that require you to adapt. Growth isn't a linear process – it's about being flexible, open to change, and willing to refine your skills as you move forward.

1. **Stay Adaptable**

    The landscape of work and business is constantly changing, and skills that were once in high demand can become obsolete. To ensure continued growth, stay adaptable and ready to learn new skills or improve existing ones.

    Actionable Tips:

    - **Identify Emerging Trends**: Stay informed about trends and technologies that could impact your industry. For example, if artificial intelligence is transforming your field, consider upskilling to remain relevant.

    - **Embrace New Challenges**: Don't shy away from opportunities that require you to step out of your comfort zone. Each new challenge is a chance to apply your skills in new ways and expand your capabilities.

2. **Commit to Lifelong Learning**

    Applying skills isn't a one-time event – it's an ongoing process. Lifelong learning is the key to staying sharp, competitive, and able to adapt as the world around you changes. By continuously improving and acquiring new skills, you open yourself to endless growth opportunities.

    Actionable Tips:

    - **Pursue Continuing Education**: Invest in ongoing education through courses, workshops, certifications, or mentorship programs that will help you stay ahead of the curve.

    - **Reflect and Reassess Regularly**: Periodically assess whether the skills in your toolkit are still relevant to your goals and industry. If not, it may be time to upskill or pivot to new areas of expertise.

Conclusion: Using Your Skills to Create a Path for Growth

The ultimate goal of acquiring and applying skills is to drive growth – whether that's personal, professional, or both. By strategically applying your skills to solve problems, add value, and create measurable impact, you position yourself for continuous success.

Growth comes from action, reflection, and adaptation. As you move forward, remember that applying your skills isn't about perfection – it's about progress. Keep learning, keep experimenting, and keep using your skills to create the outcomes that matter most to you.

In the next chapter, we'll explore how you can future-proof your skills by preparing for tomorrow's workforce and emerging industry trends.

6

Soft Skills for Success

In the modern world, where technical skills and expertise often dominate discussions about career success, soft skills—such as communication, emotional intelligence, leadership, and adaptability—are equally, if not more, important. These interpersonal and cognitive skills are what differentiate good professionals from great ones. Whether you're managing a team, collaborating with colleagues, or leading a project, soft skills help you build relationships, resolve conflicts, and create an environment where innovation and productivity thrive.

In this chapter, we'll explore the critical role soft skills play in career and personal success, why they are essential in the modern workforce, and how you can develop and apply these skills to unlock new opportunities.

What Are Soft Skills and Why Do They Matter?

Soft skills, often referred to as "people skills" or "interpersonal skills," are non-technical abilities that relate to how you interact with others and how you manage your work. While hard skills (technical expertise) are often job-specific, soft skills are transferable across roles and industries. These skills allow you to work effectively with others, manage your emotions, and navigate complex social environments.

1. **The Increasing Value of Soft Skills in the Workplace.**

   As automation and artificial intelligence continue to take over routine tasks, human workers are increasingly being relied upon for skills that machines cannot replicate: creativity, emotional intelligence, problem-solving, and adaptability. Employers today value employees who can not only perform their technical duties but also collaborate effectively, lead teams, and think critically.

2. **Soft Skills as a Differentiator**

   In a competitive job market, technical expertise alone is often not enough to stand out. Employers are looking for individuals who bring both technical know-how and strong interpersonal skills to the table. Soft skills are often the deciding factor between 2 equally qualified candidates, as they enable you to build relationships, influence others, and thrive in a collaborative environment.

   Example:

   Imagine two data analysts, both highly skilled in data manipulation and visualization. One has strong communication skills and can explain complex data insights in simple terms to non-technical stakeholders. The other struggles to communicate their findings effectively. In a business context, the analyst with stronger communication skills will have a greater impact, as they can bridge the gap between technical expertise and actionable business insights.

The Most Critical Soft Skills for Success

While there are numerous soft skills, a few are consistently highlighted as being essential for success in today's world. These are the skills that will help you not only excel in your job but also navigate the complexities of modern workplaces.

1. **Communication Skills**

   Effective communication is the foundation of all successful relationships, both personal and professional. Whether you're presenting to a group, writing an email, or giving feedback to a colleague, the ability to convey your ideas clearly and persuasively is crucial.

   Actionable Tips:

   - **Practice Active Listening**: Listening is just as important as speaking. Pay full attention when others are speaking, avoid interrupting, and ask clarifying questions to ensure understanding.

- **Tailor Your Message**: Different audiences require different communication styles. Practice adjusting your communication depending on whether you're speaking to a peer, manager, or client.

- **Master Non-Verbal Communication**: Your body language, facial expressions, and tone of voice all contribute to how your message is received. Practice maintaining open body language and making eye contact to reinforce your verbal message.

2. **Emotional Intelligence (EQ)**

Emotional intelligence is the ability to understand and manage your own emotions, as well as recognize and influence the emotions of others. High emotional intelligence allows you to navigate social complexities, maintain strong relationships, and resolve conflicts effectively.

Actionable Tips:

- **Improve Self-Awareness**: Reflect on your emotional triggers and how you react in various situations. Understanding your emotional patterns is the first step to managing them.

- **Practice Empathy**: Put yourself in others' shoes to better understand their perspectives and feelings. Empathy helps you build trust and rapport with others.

- **Manage Stress**: Emotionally intelligent individuals are skilled at managing their emotions in high-stress situations. Practice stress relief techniques such as mindfulness, deep breathing, or taking short breaks when needed.

3. **Leadership and Teamwork**

Whether or not you're in a formal leadership position, leadership skills are critical in any role. Leadership involves taking initiative, motivating others, and driving progress toward a common goal. Teamwork, on the other hand, is about working collaboratively, respecting diverse perspectives, and contributing to collective success.

Actionable Tips:

- **Take Initiative**: Volunteer for leadership roles in projects or tasks, even if they are small. Leadership is about taking responsibility and guiding others toward success.

- **Foster Collaboration**: Encourage open communication, respect others' opinions, and be proactive in resolving conflicts within your team.

- **Lead by Example**: Effective leaders model the behaviors they expect from their team. Whether it's integrity, dedication, or collaboration, demonstrate the qualities you want to inspire in others.

4. **Adaptability and Flexibility**

In today's fast-paced world, the ability to adapt to change and remain flexible in the face of uncertainty is a key skill. Employers need individuals who can pivot when new challenges arise, embrace new technologies, and learn from failure without getting discouraged.

Actionable Tips:

- **Be Open to Change**: Instead of resisting change, practice seeing it as an opportunity for growth. Adaptability requires a willingness to try new things and step out of your comfort zone.

- **Cultivate a growth mindset**: A growth mindset, where you view challenges as learning opportunities, will help you stay resilient in the face of setbacks and open to continuous development.

- **Embrace Lifelong Learning**: Adaptable individuals are always learning. Stay up-to-date with industry trends and be proactive about upskilling to remain relevant in your field.

5. **Problem-Solving and Critical Thinking**

Problem-solving involves the ability to assess a situation, think critically, and come up with effective solutions. Employers seek individuals who can approach challenges analytically, break down complex problems, and offer innovative solutions.

Actionable Tips:

- **Analyze the Problem Thoroughly**: Don't rush into solving a problem. Take time to understand the root causes and gather all relevant information before jumping to conclusions.

- **Think Creatively**: Look beyond the obvious solutions. Practice thinking creatively by considering alternative perspectives or brainstorming with others.

- **Use Structured Frameworks**: When tackling complex problems, use structured problem-solving frameworks like root cause analysis, SWOT analysis, or the 5 Whys method to guide your thinking.

Why Soft Skills Are Essential for Leadership

Leaders today need more than just technical expertise to succeed. In fact, soft skills are often the key differentiator between a manager and a true leader. Leaders who possess strong soft skills are better at building trust, inspiring their teams, and navigating complex interpersonal dynamics.

1. **Building and Leading Effective Teams**

    A leader's ability to communicate, empathize, and foster collaboration is what turns a group of individuals into a cohesive team. By understanding the strengths and weaknesses of team members, leaders can delegate tasks effectively, resolve conflicts, and create an environment where everyone can thrive.

2. **Navigating Change and Uncertainty**

    Leaders who are adaptable and emotionally intelligent can navigate change more effectively. Whether it's a business restructuring, a new technology implementation, or a global crisis, leaders with strong soft skills remain calm under pressure, provide clear direction, and support their teams through challenging times.

3. **Inspiring and Motivating Others**

    Leadership is about more than just managing tasks – it's about inspiring and motivating others to perform at their best. Leaders with strong communication skills can articulate a vision that inspires their team, while leaders with high emotional intelligence can tap into what motivates each individual, fostering loyalty and commitment.

How to Develop and Strengthen Your Soft Skills

Just like technical skills, soft skills can be developed and strengthened over time. The key is self-awareness, practice, and a willingness to seek feedback from others.

1. **Seek Feedback from Others**

    One of the best ways to improve your soft skills is by asking for feedback from colleagues, supervisors, or mentors. External perspectives can provide valuable insights into how your communication, leadership, or teamwork skills are perceived by others.

    Actionable Tips:

    -   **Ask for Specific Feedback**: Don't just ask for general feedback; request specific input on areas like communication, collaboration, or adaptability. This will give you more actionable insights to work on.

    -   **Embrace Constructive Criticism**: Feedback, especially when it's critical, can be hard to hear, but it's essential for growth. Approach feedback with an open mind and see it as an opportunity for improvement.

2. **Observe and Learn from Role Models**

    Identify leaders, colleagues, or public figures who exemplify strong soft skills. Pay attention to how they communicate, handle conflicts, or inspire their teams. Learning from others' examples can provide you with practical techniques to apply in your own interactions.

    Actionable Tips:

    -   **Shadow a Leader**: If possible, spend time observing a leader in your organization. Take note of how they handle difficult conversations, manage their time, or lead meetings.

- **Attend Workshops or Seminars**: Many organizations offer workshops or seminars on communication, leadership, and emotional intelligence. Take advantage of these opportunities to improve your soft skills.

3. **Practice in Real-Life Situations**

The best way to develop soft skills is through practice. Look for opportunities in both your professional and personal life to apply what you've learned. For example, volunteer to lead a project, mentor a colleague, or resolve a conflict within your team.

Actionable Tips:

- **Step into Leadership Roles**: Whenever possible, volunteer for leadership roles within your organization, even if it's a small team or short-term project. This will help you develop leadership, communication, and problem-solving skills.

- **Engage in Difficult Conversations**: Don't shy away from difficult conversations, whether it's giving feedback to a colleague or addressing a problem with a client. These are opportunities to practice communication and conflict resolution skills in real time.

Soft Skills in the Digital Age

As remote work and digital collaboration become more prevalent, soft skills are taking on a new dimension. In virtual environments, skills like communication, collaboration, and emotional intelligence are more critical than ever as they ensure productivity and cohesion, even when teams are not physically together.

1. **Virtual Communication**

In a digital world, the ability to communicate effectively through emails, video calls, and instant messaging platforms is crucial. Virtual communication requires clarity, brevity, and the ability to convey tone and intent without the benefit of face-to-face interaction.

Actionable Tips:

- **Be Clear and Concise**: In written communication, clarity is key. Make sure your emails and messages are clear, concise, and to the point to avoid misunderstandings.

- **Engage Actively in Meetings**: In virtual meetings, it's important to stay engaged. Make eye contact with the camera, listen actively, and contribute to the discussion to show that you're fully present.

2. **Collaboration in Virtual Teams**

Teamwork in a remote environment presents its own challenges, from time zone differences to the lack of in-person connection. Soft skills like collaboration and teamwork are essential for keeping teams aligned and productive in digital spaces.

Actionable Tips:

- **Foster Team Spirit**: Encourage virtual team-building activities to foster connection and collaboration. This could be as simple as starting meetings with an icebreaker or scheduling virtual social events.

- **Clarify Roles and Responsibilities**: In a remote setting, it's crucial to ensure that everyone understands their role within the team. This helps avoid confusion and ensures accountability.

Conclusion: The Power of Soft Skills in Achieving Success

Soft skills are the foundation of success in today's world. While technical expertise and hard skills are essential, it's your ability to communicate effectively, lead with empathy, adapt to change, and solve complex problems that will truly set you apart. Whether you're looking to advance in your career, lead a team, or improve your personal relationships, developing strong soft skills will open new doors and create lasting opportunities for growth.

This chapter has explored the most critical soft skills for success and provided actionable strategies for developing and strengthening them. In the next chapter, we'll discuss how to turn your skills—both technical and soft—into tangible opportunities for career advancement and personal fulfillment.

7

Curiosity - Force Behind Growth

Curiosity is a powerful engine of personal and professional development. It fuels the desire to learn, discover, and push boundaries, making it an essential trait for success in today's fast-paced world. In an era where industries, technologies, and skills are evolving rapidly, curiosity becomes the key to adaptability and lifelong learning. It's the spark that motivates you to ask questions, explore new ideas, and seek solutions to complex problems.

In this chapter, we'll explore the importance of curiosity in driving growth, how to cultivate it in your personal and professional life, and the profound impact it can have on your ability to innovate, solve problems, and stay ahead in your career.

The Role of Curiosity in Personal Growth

At its core, curiosity is a desire to understand the world around you. It's a natural instinct that drives you to seek out knowledge, challenge assumptions, and explore new possibilities. Curiosity plays a crucial role in personal growth because it pushes you beyond the status quo and into a mindset of continuous improvement.

1. **Curiosity Fuels Learning**

   Curiosity is the foundation of lifelong learning. When you're curious, learning becomes less of a necessity and more of an exciting journey. The more curious you are, the more motivated you become to explore new subjects, acquire new skills, and seek out new experiences. This ongoing thirst for knowledge keeps you mentally agile and adaptable in a rapidly changing world.

2. **Curiosity Encourages Self-Reflection**

   Curiosity isn't just about exploring the external world; it also encourages self-reflection. When you're curious about your own abilities, habits, and behaviors, you become more self-aware. This awareness is crucial for personal growth, as it helps you identify areas for improvement, set meaningful goals, and track your progress over time.

3. Curiosity Builds Confidence

As you satisfy your curiosity and learn new things, you build confidence in your ability to tackle challenges and solve problems. Each time you explore an unfamiliar topic or skill, you prove to yourself that you can adapt and grow. This increased confidence not only improves your personal development but also empowers you to take on bigger challenges and step outside your comfort zone.

The Role of Curiosity in Professional Success

Curiosity is equally important in the professional world. Employers value curious individuals because they are self-motivated, proactive, and capable of driving innovation. In an environment where businesses must constantly evolve to stay competitive, employees with a curious mindset can push organizations forward by exploring new ideas and finding solutions to difficult problems.

1. Curiosity Drives Innovation.

Innovation rarely happens by accident. It's driven by curiosity, by asking "what if?" and exploring new ways of doing things. In business, curious individuals challenge the status quo and seek out creative solutions to problems. They are the ones who ask why things are done a certain way, and whether there might be a better or more efficient method.

2. Curiosity Enhances Problem-Solving

Curious professionals are better equipped to solve complex problems because they aren't satisfied with surface-level answers. They dig deeper, ask more questions, and look for patterns or solutions that others may overlook. Curiosity pushes you to explore different angles and possibilities, leading to more effective and innovative solutions.

3. Curiosity Leads to Continuous Improvement

Professionals who are curious are never content with "good enough." They are always seeking ways to improve processes, optimize systems, and enhance their skills. This mindset of continuous improvement benefits both the individual and the organization, as it fosters a culture of growth and excellence.

How to Cultivate Curiosity in Your Life

While curiosity comes naturally to some, it's also a trait that can be cultivated. By adopting certain habits and mindsets, you can increase your curiosity and use it to fuel your growth.

1. Ask More Questions

One of the simplest ways to cultivate curiosity is by asking more questions. Make a habit of questioning the world around you, whether it's your work processes, your daily routines, or the information you encounter. Instead of accepting things at face value, dig deeper to understand why and how things work.

Actionable Tips:

- **Practice the 5 Whys**: When faced with a problem or situation, ask "why" 5 times to uncover the root cause or deeper meaning.

- **Be Inquisitive in Conversations**: In both professional and personal conversations, ask open-ended questions to learn more about other people's perspectives and ideas.

2. Explore New Areas of Interest

Curiosity thrives when you expose yourself to new experiences, subjects, and challenges. Make it a habit to explore areas outside of your comfort zone or expertise. This could involve learning a new skill, picking up a hobby, or diving into a topic you know little about. The more you broaden your horizons, the more opportunities you'll have to spark your curiosity.

Actionable Tips:

- **Set a Monthly Learning Goal**: Each month, commit to learning something new, whether it's reading a book on a new topic, attending a workshop, or taking an online course.

- **Challenge Yourself**: Take on projects or tasks that stretch your abilities. The process of tackling something unfamiliar will naturally ignite your curiosity.

3. Stay Open-Minded

Curiosity requires an open mind. If you approach situations with preconceived notions or rigid thinking, you limit your ability to explore new ideas. By staying open to new perspectives and possibilities, you create space for curiosity to flourish.

Actionable Tips:

- **Suspend Judgment**: When encountering new ideas or opinions, withhold your initial judgment and ask yourself, "What can I learn from this?"

- **Embrace Different Perspectives**: Engage with people who have different viewpoints, backgrounds, or expertise. Their perspectives will challenge your thinking and open you up to new ideas.

4. Embrace Failure as a Learning Tool

Curiosity often involves risk – asking questions, exploring new paths, and experimenting with different solutions. Failure is an inevitable part of this process, but it's also an opportunity for growth. By embracing failure as a learning tool, you free yourself to explore without fear of making mistakes.

Actionable Tips:

- **Experiment Regularly**: Incorporate experimentation into your work or personal life. Try new approaches and be open to the possibility of failure. View each experiment as a learning opportunity rather than a pass/fail test.

- **Reflect on Failures**: After encountering a failure or setback, take time to reflect on what you learned. Curiosity will help you uncover valuable insights from the experience.

5. **Feed Your Curiosity with Resources**

To stay curious, it's important to feed your mind with a variety of resources. Books, podcasts, documentaries, and online courses can all provide new perspectives and ideas that spark curiosity. The more you expose yourself to, the more questions you'll have – and the more motivated you'll be to seek answers.

Actionable Tips:

- **Read Widely**: Make a habit of reading about a diverse range of subjects – both related and unrelated to your field. Books, blogs, and articles can all provide new insights and ideas that inspire curiosity.

- **Follow Your Interests**: When something piques your interest, dive deeper. Whether it's an intriguing concept, a new technology, or a historical event, follow the thread of curiosity and learn as much as you can.

The Impact of Curiosity on Problem-Solving and Innovation

Curiosity is one of the driving forces behind problem-solving and innovation. When you're curious, you're not satisfied with superficial answers or standard solutions. You're driven to dig deeper, explore new ideas, and experiment with different approaches. This mindset fosters creativity and innovation, allowing you to solve problems more effectively and push the boundaries of what's possible.

1. **Curiosity Leads to Creative Solutions**

Curiosity pushes you to think outside the box and consider alternative solutions. Instead of relying on tried-and-true methods, curious individuals are willing to explore new ideas and experiment with unconventional approaches. This creative mindset is crucial in industries that demand constant innovation.

2. Curiosity Encourages Iteration

Curious problem-solvers aren't satisfied with the first solution they find. They are driven to iterate, test, and refine their ideas until they arrive at the best possible solution. This iterative mindset is especially valuable in industries like tech, where rapid prototyping and continuous improvement are key to success.

3. Curiosity Creates Breakthroughs

Some of the greatest breakthroughs in history were the result of curiosity – scientists, inventors, and entrepreneurs who asked "what if?" and pursued their curiosity to create something entirely new. By cultivating curiosity in your own life, you open yourself up to the possibility of making breakthroughs in your career, your business, or your personal growth.

Conclusion: Nurturing Curiosity for a Lifetime of Growth

Curiosity is one of the most powerful traits you can cultivate for personal and professional growth. It drives learning, fuels innovation, and empowers you to solve problems in creative and effective ways. By embracing curiosity, you open yourself up to a world of possibilities, pushing beyond limitations and discovering new paths forward.

This chapter has explored the role of curiosity in learning, problem-solving, and professional success and provided practical strategies for cultivating curiosity in your life. In the next chapter, we'll discuss how to tie everything together—practical skills, soft skills, curiosity, and adaptability—into a long-term strategy for success.

8

Accountability: The Foundation of Success

Accountability is a foundational element of success in both personal and professional life. It is the principle of being responsible for your actions, decisions, and outcomes and ensuring that you follow through on your commitments. When you are accountable, you take ownership of your results—both good and bad—and are willing to put in the effort to improve and learn from your experiences.

In this chapter, we'll explore the concept of accountability, why it is essential for personal growth and career advancement, and how to build a mindset of accountability in your daily life. We'll also look at how accountability fosters trust, boosts performance, and ultimately drives success.

What is Accountability?

Accountability goes beyond simply completing tasks or meeting deadlines. It is a proactive approach to responsibility where you take ownership of the entire process—from setting goals to achieving results and reflecting on outcomes. It means being dependable, reliable, and answerable for your actions and their consequences.

1. **Personal Accountability**

   Personal accountability refers to taking responsibility for your own actions, behaviors, and decisions. It involves recognizing that you are in control of your choices and accepting the consequences of those choices, whether positive or negative. Personal accountability drives self-discipline and fosters personal growth.

   Example:

   A person practicing personal accountability might set a goal to exercise regularly. If they miss a workout, they don't blame external factors, such as a busy schedule or poor weather. Instead, they acknowledge their role in the situation and adjust their behavior to stay on track.

2. **Professional Accountability**

In the workplace, professional accountability means owning your responsibilities, delivering on your commitments, and being transparent about your progress. It's about maintaining a standard of excellence in your work and contributing to the overall success of your team or organization.

Example:

In a professional setting, an accountable team member who misses a project deadline will communicate the reasons why it happened, take steps to mitigate the delay, and ensure that it doesn't happen again. They take responsibility rather than deflecting blame onto others.

Why Accountability is Crucial for Success

Accountability is more than just a virtue – it is a practical tool that directly impacts your ability to succeed. Whether you're working toward personal goals, career ambitions, or team objectives, accountability is the glue that holds everything together.

1. **Accountability Builds Trust**

Accountability fosters trust between individuals, teams, and organizations. When you consistently follow through on your promises, meet deadlines, and own your outcomes, others come to rely on you. This trust is essential for building strong relationships, whether with colleagues, managers, clients, or friends.

Example:

In a workplace setting, a manager who consistently holds themselves accountable creates a culture of trust. Their team knows they can count on the manager to provide support, give honest feedback, and take responsibility for decisions. This trust makes the team more cohesive and productive.

2. Accountability Increases Productivity

When you hold yourself accountable, you're more likely to stay focused and committed to your tasks. Accountability encourages you to set clear goals, monitor your progress, and prioritize your time effectively. As a result, productivity increases, and you are able to achieve more in less time.

Example:

If you're accountable for meeting a tight deadline at work, you're less likely to procrastinate. You'll set clear priorities, stay organized, and avoid distractions because you know that your performance is directly tied to your commitment to that deadline.

3. Accountability Encourages Continuous Improvement

Being accountable means acknowledging when things go wrong, learning from mistakes, and taking corrective action. Instead of making excuses or shifting blame, accountable individuals look for ways to improve, refine their processes, and enhance their performance. This creates a culture of continuous growth and development.

Example:

In a professional environment, a product manager might be held accountable for the launch of a new app. If the launch is delayed due to unforeseen technical issues, an accountable manager will reflect on what went wrong, identify ways to avoid similar problems in the future, and make the necessary adjustments for the next release.

4. Accountability Enhances Personal Growth

On a personal level, accountability encourages self-awareness and self-discipline. When you consistently hold yourself accountable for your actions and decisions, you build habits that support your long-term success. This personal responsibility drives personal growth and helps you stay aligned with your values and goals.

Example:

If you have a goal of learning a new skill, personal accountability ensures that you stick to a learning plan, review your progress regularly, and make adjustments as needed. If you miss a study session, you don't blame external circumstances—instead, you adjust your schedule and keep moving forward.

How to Cultivate Accountability in Your Life

Building a mindset of accountability takes practice and intentional effort. The more you incorporate accountability into your daily routine, the more natural it will become. Here are practical strategies to help you cultivate accountability in both personal and professional settings.

1. **Set Clear Goals and Expectations**

   Accountability starts with clear, measurable goals. When you know exactly what you need to achieve, it's easier to hold yourself responsible for the outcomes. Without clear expectations, it's easy to become complacent or lose focus.

   Actionable Tips:

   - **Set SMART Goals**: Make sure your goals are Specific, Measurable, Achievable, Relevant, and Time-bound. This structure gives you a clear target to aim for and makes it easier to track progress.

   - **Define Success Criteria**: Be specific about what success looks like. Whether it's meeting a project deadline, reaching a fitness goal, or mastering a new skill, define the criteria you will use to measure success.

2. **Monitor Your Progress Regularly**

   Accountability requires regular self-reflection and progress tracking. Without monitoring your progress, it's easy to lose sight of your goals or fall behind on commitments.

Actionable Tips:

- **Use Accountability Tools**: Consider using tools like calendars, task management apps, or journals to track your daily tasks and progress. Apps can help you stay on top of both personal and professional commitments.

- **Review Your Goals Weekly**: Set aside time each week to review your progress. Ask yourself: What did I accomplish this week? Where did I fall short? What can I improve moving forward?

3. **Own Your Mistakes and Learn from Them**

Being accountable means accepting responsibility when things don't go as planned. Instead of deflecting blame or making excuses, own up to your mistakes, reflect on what went wrong, and figure out how to improve next time.

Actionable Tips:

- **Acknowledge Failures Quickly**: If something goes wrong, acknowledge it immediately. Avoid the temptation to point fingers or downplay the issue.

- **Ask Reflective Questions**: After encountering a failure, ask yourself, "What could I have done differently?" and "What did I learn from this experience?" This reflection leads to improvement.

4. **Seek Feedback and Hold Yourself Accountable to Others**

Accountability doesn't have to be a solo effort. In fact, seeking feedback from others and holding yourself accountable to a mentor, peer, or manager can significantly enhance your personal and professional growth. This external accountability keeps you motivated and ensures that you stay on track.

Actionable Tips:

- **Find an Accountability Partner**: Work with someone who shares similar goals or is invested in your success. Check in regularly to discuss progress and challenges. Knowing that someone else is tracking your progress creates an extra layer of accountability.

- **Ask for Honest Feedback**: Actively seek feedback from colleagues, mentors, or friends. Honest feedback helps you identify blind spots and areas for improvement.

5. **Take Initiative and Follow Through**

Accountability means taking initiative, especially when it comes to delivering on your commitments. Don't wait for others to remind you of your responsibilities—be proactive and follow through on tasks without needing external pressure.

Actionable Tips:

- **Be Proactive in Your Work**: Take ownership of tasks and projects by anticipating what needs to be done and acting on it. For example, if you see an issue at work, take the initiative to address it rather than waiting for instructions.

- **Keep Your Promises**: Whether it's a deadline at work or a personal commitment to a friend, always follow through on your promises. If something changes and you can't deliver, communicate clearly and take responsibility.

The Impact of Accountability in Teams and Organizations

Accountability isn't just an individual trait – it's a crucial component of high-performing teams and organizations. When everyone in a team holds themselves accountable, productivity, trust, and collaboration improve dramatically. Accountability creates a culture of ownership, where each person is responsible for their contribution to the team's success.

1. **Building a Culture of Accountability**

In organizations where accountability is prioritized, everyone takes responsibility for their actions and results. This creates an environment of mutual trust, where individuals feel empowered to take ownership of their work and are confident in their ability to deliver.

2. **Accountability Enhances Team Collaboration.**

When individuals in a team are accountable, collaboration becomes more effective. Everyone knows that they can rely on their colleagues to deliver on their commitments, which fosters a sense of unity and purpose. This also reduces micromanagement, as managers trust their teams to handle responsibilities independently.

3. Holding Others Accountable with Empathy

Holding others accountable is essential for team success, but it should always be done with empathy and understanding. Rather than reprimanding someone for a missed deadline, approach the situation with curiosity and ask how you can support them in meeting their goals next time. Accountability and empathy go hand in hand to create a positive and constructive team culture.

Overcoming Challenges to Accountability

While accountability is key to success, it's not always easy to maintain. Procrastination, fear of failure, and external pressures can undermine accountability. Here's how to overcome some of the most common challenges.

1. Overcoming Procrastination

Procrastination is one of the biggest obstacles to accountability. When tasks feel overwhelming, it's tempting to put them off, leading to missed deadlines and a lack of follow-through.

Actionable Tips:

- **Break Tasks Into Smaller Steps**: Large tasks can feel intimidating, so break them down into manageable steps. This makes it easier to get started and maintain momentum.

- **Use Time Blocking**: Dedicate specific blocks of time to work on your tasks. This helps prevent procrastination and ensures that you make steady progress toward your goals.

2. Confronting Fear of Failure

Fear of failure can prevent you from holding yourself accountable, as it creates a reluctance to take risks or try new things. However, accountability and growth require the courage to face setbacks and learn from them.

3. **Actionable Tips:**

    - **Reframe Failure as Feedback**: Instead of viewing failure as a negative outcome, reframe it as valuable feedback. Each failure provides lessons that help you improve moving forward.

    - **Focus on the Process, Not Perfection**: Accountability isn't about being perfect—it's about showing up, trying your best, and learning along the way. Don't let fear of imperfection hold you back.

Conclusion: Accountability as the Foundation of Success

Accountability is one of the most powerful drivers of personal and professional success. It empowers you to take ownership of your actions, build trust with others, and continuously improve your performance. By cultivating accountability in your daily life, you lay the foundation for achieving your goals, building strong relationships, and driving long-term growth.

This chapter has explored the importance of accountability, provided strategies for developing a mindset of responsibility, and highlighted the impact of accountability on both individual success and team dynamics.

9

The Continuous Game: Lifelong Learning

In a world where skills, technologies, and industries are evolving at an unprecedented pace, lifelong learning is no longer just a choice—it's a necessity. The days of finishing school and relying on that education for the rest of your career are over. Today, the most successful individuals are those who continually seek out new knowledge, adapt to change, and enhance their skill sets. Lifelong learning isn't about formal education alone; it's about embracing a mindset of constant growth and staying curious about the world around you.

In this chapter, we will explore the importance of lifelong learning, how to develop a learning strategy, the benefits of continuous growth, and practical ways to integrate learning into your everyday life. By the end of this chapter, you'll have a clear framework for making lifelong learning a core part of your personal and professional journey.

Why Lifelong Learning Matters

Lifelong learning is the key to staying relevant, competitive, and fulfilled in a fast-changing world. It provides you with the tools to keep up with industry shifts, pivot when necessary, and take advantage of new opportunities. Here's why it's critical to your long-term success:

1. **Adapting to Rapid Change**

   Industries today are experiencing rapid shifts due to technological innovation, globalization, and market evolution. Skills that were in high demand 5 years ago may no longer be relevant, and entirely new job roles are emerging. Lifelong learners can adapt to these changes by constantly updating their knowledge and skills, making them more agile and adaptable in their careers.

2. **Staying Competitive in the Job Market**

   With industries becoming more skills-driven, companies are increasingly looking for candidates who demonstrate not only proficiency in their current skills but also the ability to learn new ones. Lifelong learners are attractive to employers because they show a commitment to growth and adaptability, both of which are crucial in a rapidly changing job market.

3. **Personal Fulfillment and Growth**

   Lifelong learning isn't just about career success – it's also about personal fulfillment. Learning new things can spark creativity, build confidence, and bring a sense of achievement. It enriches your life and keeps your mind sharp as you grow and evolve. For many, the pursuit of knowledge is a source of motivation and joy that transcends professional aspirations.

Developing a Lifelong Learning Strategy

To make lifelong learning a habit, you need a strategy that fits into your lifestyle and aligns with your goals. Developing a learning plan helps you stay focused, track progress, and continuously push yourself to grow. Here's how to build an effective lifelong learning strategy:

1. **Identify Your Learning Goals**

   The first step in developing a lifelong learning strategy is to identify what you want to learn. These goals should align with both your personal interests and your professional objectives. Ask yourself: Where do I want to grow? What new skills or knowledge do I need to achieve my goals? These questions will help you define your learning path.

   Actionable Tips:

   - **Break Down Long-Term Goals**: If you want to become a leader in your industry, break that down into specific learning goals— whether it's mastering public speaking, learning management techniques, or developing technical skills.

- **Incorporate Personal Interests**: Lifelong learning doesn't have to be all about work. Include personal interests, like learning photography, cooking, or painting, to keep your mind stimulated and balanced.

2. **Create a Learning Routine**

   To make learning a lifelong habit, you need to build it into your daily or weekly routine. Consistency is key when it comes to mastering new skills, and regular practice will lead to steady progress.

   Actionable Tips:

   - **Dedicate Time to Learning**: Whether it's 30 minutes a day or a few hours each weekend, carve out dedicated time to focus on learning. It could be reading, taking an online course, or practicing a new skill.

   - **Use Microlearning Techniques**: Microlearning involves breaking down learning into small, manageable chunks. This could be reading an article, watching a short tutorial, or completing a daily challenge. This approach helps you make progress without feeling overwhelmed.

3. **Leverage Multiple Learning Sources**

   Lifelong learning doesn't happen in one place—it comes from a variety of sources. The key is to diversify where and how you learn. This could include formal education, online courses, mentorship, podcasts, reading, and hands-on experience.

   Actionable Tips:

   - **Online Learning Platforms**: Use platforms like Coursera, Udemy, or LinkedIn Learning to access a wide variety of courses on both technical and soft skills. Many of these platforms offer certifications that can also enhance your resume.

   - **Podcasts and Audiobooks**: Use your commute, workout, or downtime to listen to educational podcasts or audiobooks that align with your learning goals.

   - **Books and Articles**: Develop a habit of reading regularly. Industry books, research papers, and blogs offer valuable insights that keep you updated with the latest trends and best practices.

4. **Measure and Track Progress**

Learning should be intentional and measurable. By tracking your progress, you can identify where you're excelling and where you need to focus more attention. This will also help you stay motivated as you see tangible results from your learning efforts.

Actionable Tips:

- **Set Milestones**: Break your learning journey into milestones. For example, if you're learning a new programming language, aim to complete a certain number of projects or solve a set number of coding challenges within a given timeframe.

- **Use Learning Journals**: Keep a learning journal where you reflect on what you've learned, how you've applied it, and what you want to explore next. This will help reinforce new knowledge and track your learning over time.

The Benefits of Lifelong Learning

While the need for lifelong learning is clear, it's also important to understand the tangible benefits that come with continuous growth. From career advancement to personal well-being, lifelong learning enriches many areas of life.

1. **Increased Career Opportunities**

   One of the most obvious benefits of lifelong learning is the career opportunities it opens up. Staying current with industry trends, learning new technologies, and refining your skills make you more attractive to employers and increase your chances of promotion, salary increases, and new job offers.

2. **Enhanced Problem-Solving Abilities**

   Lifelong learners are better equipped to tackle challenges and solve problems. As you acquire new skills and knowledge, you build a mental toolkit that allows you to approach problems from different angles and find innovative solutions.

3. Personal Satisfaction and Confidence

Learning new things gives you a sense of accomplishment that can boost your self-esteem and overall confidence. This feeling of progress—whether it's mastering a new language, developing a technical skill, or becoming a better leader—translates into other areas of life, empowering you to take on bigger challenges.

4. Cognitive Health and Longevity

Lifelong learning has been shown to improve cognitive health and potentially delay the onset of cognitive decline. Engaging in continuous intellectual stimulation keeps your brain active, improving memory, problem-solving, and critical thinking skills as you age.

Overcoming Challenges to Lifelong Learning

While lifelong learning is incredibly valuable, it's not always easy. Many people face barriers such as time constraints, financial limitations, or a lack of motivation. Here are some strategies for overcoming these challenges:

1. Time Management

One of the biggest barriers to lifelong learning is finding the time. Balancing work, family, and other responsibilities can make it difficult to dedicate time to learning. The solution lies in effective time management and prioritization.

Actionable Tips:

- **Incorporate Learning Into Daily Routines**: Listen to podcasts or audiobooks during your commute, workout, or while doing household chores.

- **Use the Pomodoro Technique**: Break down learning sessions into manageable time blocks (e.g. 25 minutes of focused learning followed by a 5-minute break). This method keeps you productive without feeling overwhelmed.

2. Financial Constraints

Not all learning opportunities are free, and formal education or advanced certifications can be expensive. However, there are numerous free or low-cost alternatives available that can still provide high-quality learning experiences.

Actionable Tips:

- **Utilize Free Learning Resources**: Websites offer free lessons and tutorials on a wide variety of subjects.

- **Apply for Scholarships or Grants**: Many organizations and educational institutions offer financial aid, grants, or scholarships for professional development and education.

3. **Maintaining Motivation**

Staying motivated to keep learning can be a challenge, especially when progress feels slow or when life gets busy. To maintain motivation, it's important to set clear goals, celebrate small victories, and remind yourself of the long-term benefits of learning.

Actionable Tips:

- **Join Learning Communities**: Being part of a learning group or online community can provide motivation and accountability. Platforms often have communities focused on specific topics or industries.

- **Reward Yourself**: Set up a reward system for yourself. For example, after completing a course or learning a new skill, treat yourself to something you enjoy as a way to celebrate your achievement.

Conclusion: A Lifelong Commitment to Growth.

Lifelong learning is not just a strategy for staying relevant in a rapidly changing world—it's a mindset and a lifestyle. It's about being curious, continuously improving, and embracing change as an opportunity for growth. By adopting a lifelong learning strategy, you will equip yourself with the skills, knowledge, and adaptability needed to succeed in any industry or personal endeavor.

This chapter has outlined the importance of lifelong learning, how to develop a learning strategy, and how to integrate learning into your daily life. In the next chapter, we will explore how to apply the skills you've learned to create measurable success in both your personal and professional life.

10

Turning Skills Into Opportunities

The skills you acquire are valuable assets, but their true power is unlocked when you use them to create opportunities for growth, advancement, and fulfillment. Whether it's landing your dream job, starting a business, or making an impact in your current role, the ability to turn your skills into real-world opportunities is what sets successful people apart.

In this chapter, we'll explore how to leverage your skills strategically to seize opportunities, build a strong personal brand, network effectively, and continuously expand your professional reach. By the end of this chapter, you will have a roadmap for turning your skills into tangible opportunities that propel your career and personal aspirations forward.

The Power of Skills in Creating Opportunities

Your skills are like tools in a toolbox. While having them is essential, knowing how to use them effectively in the right situations is what leads to success. The key to turning your skills into opportunities lies in identifying when and where to apply them to create value, solve problems, and open new doors.

1. **Recognizing Opportunities in Everyday Situations**

   Opportunities often come disguised as challenges or routine tasks. The ability to recognize these as opportunities for growth or career advancement is a skill in itself. When you approach your work with a proactive mindset and an eye for innovation, even small tasks can become opportunities to showcase your abilities and create impact.

   Actionable Tips:

   - **Look for Unmet Needs**: In your current job or personal life, look for gaps where your skills can make a difference. Is there a process that can be improved? A problem that needs solving? By stepping up and offering solutions, you position yourself as a problem-solver.

- **Take Initiative**: Don't wait for someone to ask you to use your skills—look for ways to proactively apply them. Whether it's offering to lead a project, suggesting a new idea, or helping a colleague, taking initiative creates opportunities to demonstrate your value.

2. **Adding Value Through Your Skills**

Creating value is the most effective way to turn your skills into opportunities. The more value you provide to others—whether it's your employer, clients, or colleagues—the more doors will open for you. Value can come in many forms: improving efficiency, solving problems, increasing revenue, or delivering outstanding service.

Actionable Tips:

- **Solve Problems Others Can't**: Identify areas where your unique skills can solve complex or persistent problems

- **Show Results**: Always focus on results. When you apply your skills, make sure there's a measurable impact—whether it's saving time, increasing sales, or improving team productivity. Tangible outcomes demonstrate the value you bring to the table.

Building a Personal Brand Around Your Skills

In today's digital world, building a strong personal brand is essential for standing out and turning your skills into career opportunities. Your personal brand is how you present yourself to the world—it's a reflection of your expertise, values, and what you bring to the table.

1. **Define Your Unique Value Proposition**

To build a strong personal brand, start by defining your unique value proposition. This is a clear statement of the specific skills, expertise, and qualities that set you apart from others. It should answer the question: What do you do better than anyone else?

Actionable Tips:

- **Identify Your Core Strengths**: Reflect on your skills and experiences to identify what you're best at and how these skills provide value. Are you an expert at simplifying complex problems? Are you a creative thinker who generates innovative solutions?

- **Align with Your Goals**: Ensure your personal brand aligns with your long-term career goals. For example, if you're looking to advance into a leadership role, emphasize your leadership and communication skills in your brand.

2. Showcase Your Skills Online

In the digital age, an online presence is crucial for turning skills into opportunities. Building a strong online brand allows you to showcase your expertise, connect with industry leaders, and position yourself as a thought leader in your field.

Actionable Tips:

- **Leverage LinkedIn**: Make sure your LinkedIn profile is up-to-date, with a clear headline that highlights your key skills and a summary that tells your career story. Share articles, achievements, and projects that demonstrate your expertise.

- **Create a Portfolio**: If your work involves creative or technical skills, create an online portfolio that showcases your best projects. This could be a personal website or a platform like Behance for designers or GitHub for developers.

- **Engage in Industry Conversations**: Join online communities, participate in discussions on platforms like Twitter or Reddit, and engage with thought leaders in your industry. By contributing to conversations, you increase your visibility and credibility.

3. Build Credibility Through Content

Creating content is one of the most effective ways to establish credibility and demonstrate your skills. Whether it's writing blog posts, recording podcasts, or speaking at events, sharing your knowledge publicly can position you as an expert and open up new opportunities.

Actionable Tips:

- **Start Blogging**: Write articles that showcase your expertise and share insights from your experiences. Blogging is a great way to demonstrate your knowledge and attract attention from employers, clients, or industry leaders.

- **Create Video Content**: If writing isn't your strength, consider creating video content to share your insights. Platforms like YouTube or LinkedIn Video are great ways to reach a wider audience.

- **Speak at Industry Events**: Look for opportunities to speak at conferences, webinars, or local meetups. Public speaking is a powerful way to showcase your expertise and connect with others in your field.

Networking and Expanding Your Professional Reach

Networking is one of the most important ways to turn your skills into career opportunities. The relationships you build can lead to job offers, business collaborations, and mentorships that propel your career forward. Effective networking isn't just about collecting contacts – it's about building meaningful relationships based on mutual value.

1. **The Power of Networking**

   Networking is about creating connections that can help you advance your career, open doors to new opportunities, and expose you to different perspectives. A strong network can provide you with access to resources, advice, and job leads that you may not find on your own.

   Actionable Tips:

   - **Attend Industry Events**: Whether online or in person, attend conferences, workshops, or meetups where you can meet people in your field. These events are great places to expand your network and learn about new opportunities.

- **Engage in Online Communities**: Platforms offer opportunities to connect with professionals around the world. Be active in discussions, share your insights, and build relationships with like-minded people.

2. **Building Meaningful Connections**

Networking is not just about collecting business cards or LinkedIn connections—it's about building genuine, meaningful relationships. To do this, you need to focus on giving as much as you get. Approach networking with the mindset of creating value for others, and opportunities will follow.

Actionable Tips:

- **Offer Help First**: When networking, always look for ways you can help others before asking for something in return. This builds goodwill and makes people more likely to reciprocate.

- **Follow Up and Stay in Touch**: After meeting someone, follow up with a personalized message to reinforce the connection. Regularly check in with your contacts to maintain the relationship, even when you don't need anything from them.

3. **Finding Mentors and Sponsors**

Mentorship can be a powerful way to turn your skills into opportunities. A mentor can guide you in your career, help you develop new skills, and introduce you to important connections. Sponsors, on the other hand, are individuals who actively advocate for you, putting your name forward for promotions or new opportunities.

Actionable Tips:

- **Seek Out Mentors**: Look for people who are where you want to be in your career and ask them for guidance. Most people are willing to mentor if you show a genuine desire to learn and grow.

- **Build Relationships with Sponsors**: Sponsors are often people in leadership roles who have influence in your field. Build relationships with these individuals by consistently delivering excellent work and demonstrating your value.

Leveraging Skills for Career Advancement

Turning your skills into career advancement requires not only applying them effectively but also positioning yourself for promotions and new opportunities. Whether you're looking to move up in your current company or transition to a new role, strategically using your skills can help you stand out and accelerate your career growth.

1. **Showcase Your Skills to Decision-Makers**

   If you're aiming for a promotion or new responsibility, it's essential that the right people are aware of your capabilities. This means making your skills and accomplishments visible to decision-makers within your organization or industry.

   Actionable Tips:

   - **Take on High-Visibility Projects**: Seek out projects that will put you in front of key decision-makers. Volunteer for initiatives that are aligned with the company's goals and that allow you to demonstrate your leadership, problem-solving, or technical expertise.

   - **Share Your Achievements**: Don't assume that your achievements will be noticed on their own. Make sure to communicate your accomplishments to your supervisors in a professional manner, such as in one-on-one meetings or performance reviews.

2. **Position Yourself as a Leader**

   Leadership skills are highly valued by employers, even if you're not in a formal leadership role. Demonstrating leadership qualities—such as taking initiative, mentoring colleagues, or driving innovation— can position you for advancement.

   Actionable Tips:

   - **Lead from Any Position**: Leadership isn't about having a title; it's about influence and initiative. Look for opportunities to take the lead on projects, help your team navigate challenges, or propose new ideas that improve the company.

- **Develop Others**: Helping your colleagues grow by sharing your skills and knowledge demonstrates leadership and creates a positive impact on the team. It also positions you as someone who is capable of managing people in the future.

3. **Negotiate for New Opportunities**

   When you've proven your value through your skills and accomplishments, it's important to advocate for yourself. Negotiating for a promotion, raise, or new responsibility can be intimidating, but it's a critical step in turning your skills into tangible rewards.

   Actionable Tips:

   - **Prepare Your Case**: Before entering a negotiation, be prepared to articulate the value you bring to the organization. Highlight specific examples of how your skills have contributed to success—whether through increased revenue, improved efficiency, or leadership.

   - **Be Confident and Professional**: Confidence is key when negotiating. Be clear about what you're asking for and back up your request with evidence of your impact. Keep the conversation professional and focused on how your skills align with the company's goals.

Taking the Leap: Turning Skills Into Entrepreneurship

For many, the ultimate goal of turning skills into opportunities is entrepreneurship. If you've developed valuable skills, you may want to leverage them to start your own business, become a consultant, or launch a side project that brings you both fulfillment and financial independence.

1. **Identify a Market Need**

   The first step in turning your skills into a business is identifying a market need that aligns with your expertise. This means finding a problem that your skills can solve, whether for individuals or businesses.

Actionable Tips:

- **Research the Market**: Look for gaps in the market where your skills can provide a solution. This could be anything from offering a specialized service to creating a product that addresses unmet needs.

- **Validate Your Idea**: Before investing time and money into your business, validate your idea by testing it with potential customers. This could involve offering your services on a freelance basis or creating a minimum viable product (MVP) to gauge interest.

2. Build Your Brand as an Entrepreneur

Once you've identified a business opportunity, building a strong personal and professional brand is crucial to your success as an entrepreneur. Your brand will help you attract clients, differentiate yourself from competitors, and establish credibility in your industry.

Actionable Tips:

- **Create a Website**: Your website is your online storefront. It should clearly communicate what you do, who you serve, and the value you provide. Make sure to showcase your skills, experience, and portfolio.

- **Leverage Social Media**: Use social media platforms like LinkedIn, Instagram, or Twitter to promote your business, share content, and engage with potential customers.

3. Start Small and Scale

If you're unsure about diving into entrepreneurship full-time, start small. Many successful businesses begin as side projects or freelance gigs. This allows you to test your idea, build your brand, and gain experience without the financial risk of leaving your current job.

Actionable Tips:

- **Offer Your Services as a Freelancer**: If you're skilled in graphic design, writing, or web development, start by offering your services on freelance platforms like Upwork or Fiverr.

- **Build a Side Project**: If you're not ready to launch a full business, work on a side project that allows you to apply your skills. This could be anything from starting a blog to developing a mobile app.

Conclusion: Creating a Future of Endless Opportunities

Turning your skills into opportunities is not just about being good at what you do – it's about knowing how to position yourself, showcase your value, and seize the right moments to apply your expertise. Whether you're looking to climb the corporate ladder, start your own business, or create meaningful impact in your current role, the skills you've developed are your most powerful asset.

This chapter has provided you with actionable strategies for leveraging your skills to create opportunities for growth and success. In the next chapter, we'll explore how to prepare for the ever-changing future of work and ensure your skills remain relevant in an evolving world.

11

The Future of Skills

In an era defined by rapid technological advancements and ever-evolving industries, one thing is clear: the skills that are crucial today may not be relevant tomorrow. As automation, artificial intelligence, and digital transformation continue to reshape the job market, the future of work is uncertain, but one thing remains constant – the need for adaptability and continuous learning.

In this chapter, we will explore the emerging skills that are becoming essential across industries, the role of technology in shaping the future of work, and how you can future-proof yourself by continuously updating and refining your skills. By the end of this chapter, you will have a roadmap for staying ahead of the curve in a world that's changing faster than ever before.

The Future of Work: A Landscape in Transition

The future of work is not a distant concept—it's already unfolding before our eyes. Technologies like artificial intelligence (AI), machine learning, blockchain, and automation are fundamentally transforming industries, reshaping job roles, and creating entirely new career paths. As a result, the skills that employers seek are evolving at an unprecedented pace.

1. **Automation and AI**

   Automation and AI are no longer future trends – they are part of the present reality. From manufacturing and logistics to finance and healthcare, AI-driven automation is revolutionizing processes, optimizing operations, and making human workers more efficient. While some jobs will be automated, many new roles will emerge that require humans to manage, interpret, and enhance AI systems.

   For example, jobs in AI development, data science, and machine learning are rapidly expanding. Moreover, soft skills like emotional intelligence, creativity, and complex problem-solving—skills that cannot be easily automated—are becoming even more valuable.

2. The Gig Economy and Remote Work

The gig economy and remote work have already transformed the traditional 9-to-5 work model, with freelance platforms and remote tools making it easier for individuals to work from anywhere. This shift is expected to continue, leading to a decentralized workforce where skills, rather than geographical location, are the primary criteria for success.

3. Industry 4.0 and Digital Transformation

Industry 4.0 refers to the current trend of automation and data exchange in manufacturing and industrial technologies. It includes concepts like the Internet of Things (IoT), cloud computing, and smart factories. As digital transformation continues to impact industries, workers will need to develop the technical and digital skills required to thrive in this new environment.

Emerging Skills for the Future

The future of work will demand a combination of technical and soft skills. While technical skills will be necessary to navigate and work with new technologies, soft skills will play a critical role in enabling individuals to adapt, collaborate, and lead in a tech-driven world.

1. Digital Literacy and Data Fluency

As the world becomes increasingly digital, being proficient in digital tools and platforms is no longer optional—it's essential. Digital literacy involves the ability to navigate online environments, use cloud-based tools, and work with digital systems efficiently. In addition, data fluency, or the ability to interpret, analyze, and draw insights from data, is becoming a core skill in industries ranging from marketing to healthcare.

Actionable Tips:

- **Build Your Digital Toolbox**: Familiarize yourself with essential digital tools.

- **Learn Basic Data Skills**: Whether you're in marketing, finance, or management, learning basic data analytics will be crucial for making data-driven decisions.

2. **Artificial Intelligence (AI) and Machine Learning (ML)**

As AI and machine learning become integral to more industries, understanding how these technologies work will be a major advantage. Even if you're not in a technical role, knowing how to leverage AI tools to optimize your work can set you apart.

Actionable Tips:

- **Take Introductory AI and ML Courses**: Platforms offer beginner courses in AI and ML. Even a basic understanding of these technologies can help you stay relevant.

- **Explore AI Tools in Your Field**: Every industry is starting to incorporate AI tools. Learn how your industry is using AI and familiarize yourself with key platforms and software.

3. **Adaptability and Learning Agility**

The pace of change in the workforce means that skills you develop today may become obsolete in a few years. This is why adaptability—the ability to learn new things quickly and pivot when needed—is becoming one of the most important traits for the future workforce.

Actionable Tips:

- **Embrace Lifelong Learning**: Commit to continuous learning by attending workshops, conferences, or enrolling in online courses.

- **Practice Flexibility**: Try to be open to new roles, challenges, and projects. Being able to pivot in your career is essential for long-term success in a constantly evolving world.

4. **Critical Thinking and Problem-Solving**

As machines handle more routine tasks, human workers will increasingly be called upon to solve complex problems, make strategic decisions, and think critically. The ability to evaluate information, analyze scenarios, and come up with innovative solutions will be invaluable in the workforce of the future.

Actionable Tips:

- **Cultivate a Problem-Solving Mindset**: Practice approaching problems methodically by identifying root causes, evaluating potential solutions, and iterating based on feedback.

- **Take on Complex Projects**: Look for opportunities at work or in personal projects that require you to navigate ambiguity and solve problems creatively.

5. **Emotional Intelligence and Interpersonal Skills**

With the rise of automation, skills that involve human interaction and emotional intelligence will be irreplaceable. Emotional intelligence (EQ) is the ability to understand and manage your emotions, as well as recognize and influence the emotions of others. As the workplace becomes more collaborative, having strong interpersonal and communication skills will be crucial for success.

Actionable Tips:

- **Improve Your Self-Awareness**: Reflect regularly on how your emotions and behaviors affect others, and practice active listening.

- **Build Strong Relationships**: Work on building genuine connections with colleagues, clients, and partners. Strong relationships are key to collaborative success.

How to Future-Proof Your Skills

Future-proofing your skills means staying ahead of industry trends and continually upgrading your abilities to remain competitive. Here's how you can prepare yourself for the skills-driven future.

1. **Embrace Continuous Learning**

The most successful individuals are those who commit to lifelong learning. As new technologies and methods emerge, the need to stay up-to-date will be more critical than ever. Adopting a growth mindset—where you see learning as an ongoing process—will help you thrive in the future of work.

Actionable Tips:

- **Schedule Learning Time**: Dedicate specific time each week to learning, whether it's reading industry publications, taking an online course, or listening to podcasts.

- **Diversify Your Skillset**: Don't limit your learning to one area. Building skills across various disciplines—such as tech, leadership, communication, and strategy—will make you more adaptable and versatile.

2. Build a Personal Brand Around Your Skills

A strong personal brand is your unique identity that differentiates you from others in your field. As work becomes more decentralized and remote, having a personal brand that highlights your skills and expertise will be crucial for standing out in a crowded marketplace.

Actionable Tips:

- **Create a Portfolio**: Showcase your skills, projects, and achievements in a personal portfolio, whether that's through a personal website, a blog, or a LinkedIn profile.

- **Share Your Knowledge**: Contribute to your industry by writing articles, speaking at events, or creating content on platforms like LinkedIn. Sharing your expertise helps establish you as a thought leader.

3. Develop Cross-Disciplinary Knowledge

Specialization is important, but having cross-disciplinary knowledge will make you more flexible and adaptable to future roles. The ability to combine knowledge from different fields—such as technology, business, and the arts—will make you a more innovative problem-solver.

Actionable Tips:

- **Learn Beyond Your Field**: Take time to study topics outside your primary area of expertise. For example, if you're in marketing, learning about psychology or data science could give you a unique edge.

- **Collaborate with Diverse Teams:** Working with people from different backgrounds or industries helps you learn how to apply your skills in new ways and gain fresh perspectives.

Navigating the Future Workforce

The future workforce will likely be more decentralized, with individuals working remotely, collaborating across time zones, and even engaging in freelance or gig-based work. Here are key strategies for thriving in this evolving landscape.

1. **Master Remote Collaboration Tools**

   As remote work becomes more common, knowing how to effectively collaborate with distributed teams will be essential. Many tools are now standard in many workplaces, and mastering them will enhance your productivity and communication skills.

2. **Build a Global Network**

   The future workforce will be increasingly global, and building a diverse network of connections from different countries and industries will be a valuable asset. Networking globally opens doors to new opportunities, collaborations, and learning experiences.

The Skills Economy: What to Expect

The skills economy refers to a world where skills—rather than traditional qualifications or degrees—are the primary currency. In this future, workers will need to constantly refine their abilities to remain competitive and employable. Here's what to expect:

1. **Skills-Based Hiring**

   More companies are shifting toward skills-based hiring, where candidates are evaluated based on their practical abilities rather than their degrees. Platforms like LinkedIn are integrating skills assessments, and some companies now require job applicants to complete skill tests rather than just submitting resumes.

2. **Micro-Credentials and Certifications**

In the future, micro-credentials and certifications will play a significant role in skill validation. These are short, focused learning experiences that validate specific skills, making them attractive to employers who need proof of competency.

3. **Skill Portfolios**

Similar to how creatives maintain portfolios of their work, more professionals will start building skill portfolios that demonstrate their abilities through real-world projects, case studies, and evidence of impact.

Conclusion: Preparing for Tomorrow's Workforce

The future of work is here, and it's driven by skills. By focusing on emerging technologies, embracing continuous learning, and developing a wide range of both technical and soft skills, you can future-proof your career and remain competitive in the job market.

This chapter has explored the evolving landscape of work and the skills that will define success in the coming years. By adapting to change and proactively building your skills, you'll be equipped to navigate the future workforce with confidence and resilience.

Bibliography

- Anders, Ericsson & Pool, Robert. *Peak: Secrets from the New Science of Expertise.* Mariner Books, 2017.

- Covey, Stephen R. *The 7 Habits of Highly Effective People: Powerful Lessons in Personal Change.* Free Press, 2004.

- Dweck, Carol S. *Mindset: The New Psychology of Success.* Ballantine Books, 2007.

- Duckworth, Angela. *Grit: The Power of Passion and Perseverance.* Scribner, 2016.

- Goleman, Daniel. *Emotional Intelligence: Why It Can Matter More Than IQ.* Bantam Books, 1995.

- Grant, Adam. *Think Again: The Power of Knowing What You Don't Know.* Viking, 2021.

- Newport, Calif. *Deep Work: Rules for Focused Success in a Distracted World.* Grand Central Publishing, 2016.

- Pink, Daniel H. *Drive: The Surprising Truth About What Motivates Us.* Riverhead Books, 2011.

- Sinek, Simon. *Start with Why: How Great Leaders Inspire Everyone to Take Action.* Penguin, 2009.

- Zenger, Jack & Folkman, Joseph. *The Extraordinary Leader: Turning Good Managers into Great Leaders.* McGraw-Hill, 2009.

- Brown, Brené. *Dare to Lead: Brave Work. Tough Conversations. Whole Hearts.* Random House, 2018.

- Heath, Chip & Heath, Dan. *Switch: How to Change Things When Change Is Hard.* Broadway Books, 2010.

- Leonard, George. *Mastery: The Keys to Success and Long-Term Fulfillment.* Plume, 1992.

- Sutton, Robert I. *The No Asshole Rule: Building a Civilised Workplace and Surviving One That Isn't*. Business Plus, 2007.

- Clear, James. *Atomic Habits: An Easy & Proven Way to Build Good Habits & Break Bad Ones*. Avery, 2018.

About the Author

Dushyant Bhatt is a seasoned technology leader with over 12 years of experience in building innovative products. Throughout his career, Dushyant has been driven by a passion for solving complex challenges and delivering impactful solutions across a variety of industries.

As a visionary leader, Dushyant has spearheaded the development of global products, taking ideas from concept to reality. His deep passion for exploring emerging technologies and mentoring aspiring professionals has been a cornerstone of his career, making him a highly respected figure in the tech industry.

Dushyant's contributions to the technology industry have been widely recognized. He has been honored with prestigious awards, including:

- **Best Engineering Leader of the Year**
- **CTO of the Year**
- **Innovative Tech Leader**

In addition to his professional accomplishments, Dushyant is passionate about lifelong learning, sharing his expertise, and mentoring the next generation of tech professionals. His book, *Game of Skills*, distils his vast experience into a guide aimed at helping readers take ownership of their growth and succeed in today's fast-changing world.

To learn more, visit **DushyantBhatt.in**.